STRATEGY

RECOVERY FROM A FINANCIAL CRISIS

LEKIESHA ALLEN

WESTBOW
PRESS®
A DIVISION OF THOMAS NELSON
& ZONDERVAN

WestBow Press books may be ordered through booksellers or by contacting:

WestBow Press
A Division of Thomas Nelson & Zondervan
1663 Liberty Drive
Bloomington, IN 47403
www.westbowpress.com
844-714-3454

Scripture marked (NKJV) taken from the New King James Version®. Copyright © 1982 by Thomas Nelson. Used by permission. All rights reserved.

Scripture marked (KJV) taken from the King James Version of the Bible.

ISBN: 978-1-6642-0458-4 (sc)
ISBN: 978-1-6642-0459-1 (e)

Print information available on the last page.

WestBow Press rev. date: 09/17/2020

CONTENTS

REFERENCES

www.cnbc.com/2009/04/27/Americas-
Biggest-Types-of-Debt-.html

www.google.com

New King James Bible

King James Bible

DISCLAIMER

FOR EDUCATIONAL AND INFORMATIONAL PURPOSES ONLY

The information provided in or through our Website, Programs, Products and Services is for educational and informational purposes only and is made available to you as self-help tools for your own use.

NOT LEGAL OR FINANCIAL ADVICE

The information contained in our Website, Programs, or Services is not intended to be a substitute for legal or financial advice that can be provided by your own attorney, accountant, and/or financial advisor. In good standing does not replace the guidance you would get from a financial advisor. We cannot be held responsible for any errors or omissions, and we accept no liability whatsoever for any loss or damage howsoever arising. The law varies by state, and it is constantly changing, and therefore it affects each individual and business in different ways. As a result, it is recommended to seek outside financial and/or legal counsel relating to your specific circumstances as needed. You are hereby advised to consult with your tax consultant, accountant or lawyer for any and all questions and concerns you have, may have, or hereafter have regarding your own income and taxes, and any and all information presented by our Website, Programs or Services pertaining to your specific financial and/or legal situation.

PERSONAL RESPONSIBILITY

Our Website, Programs, Products, and Services aim to accurately represent the information provided. You are acknowledging that you are participating voluntarily in using our Website, Programs, Products, and Services, and you alone are solely and personally responsible for your results. You agree to use your own due diligence and judgment before applying any recommendation or advice that you may receive on or through our Website, Programs, Products, and Services. You acknowledge that you take full responsibility for your health, life, and well-being and for all decisions now and in the future.

NO GUARANTEES

My role is to educate, support, and assist you in reaching your own goals, but your success depends solely on your own effort, dedication, and follow-through. We cannot predict that you will attain a particular result, and you accept and understand that results are different for each individual. You fully agree that there are no guarantees as to the specific outcome or results you can expect from using the information you receive on or through this Website.

NO ENDORSEMENT

References or links in my Website to the information, opinions, advice, programs, products or services of any other individual, business or entity does not constitute my formal endorsement. We are merely sharing this information as a self-help resource only. I am not responsible for the website content, blogs, e-mails, videos, social media, programs, products and/or services of any other person, business or entity that may be linked or referenced on our Information or Website. Conversely, should my Website link appear in any other individual's, business's or entity's website, program, product or services, it does not constitute my formal endorsement of them, their business or their website either.

INTRODUCTION

Strategy was written to inspire people to become financially free through Jesus Christ.

Recovering from your Financial Crisis can come in many forms. First you have to identify what caused the financial crises in the first place. Every crisis don't have the same origin. For some it is the loss of a spouse, health issues, job loss, back problems in which you are now limited. Whatever the circumstances are people have financial problems in one way or another. Take a moment to think about what your financial crisis. Can you identify what is happening to you financially? Well, this source was written to let you know Jesus Christ would like to help you recover from your financial crisis. Debts and bills become shackles after a certain amount of time. You might be asking what shackle? Or what is a shackle? The word shackle has many different meanings but the key meanings I would like to focus on are to: "restrain, restrict, limit, constrain, handicap or hinder" (Source: Google.com). Let's go deeper so you can get an idea of what you need to do to be financially free and break your shackles.

WHAT IS REAL FINANCIAL FREEDOM?

When you think of Financial Freedom you think of not having to work any longer, having money in the bank, a pretty house with a white picket fence, a three car garage, absolutely not a bill in the world or a care in the world. Don't get me wrong, that's a good, positive way to think. But that's not the only aspect to financial freedom. It comes in many forms.

Think about your source of income, for instance. Whether it's a job, SSI, child support, whatever your source is. How long have you been there? Are you receiving your worth? Is it a dead end? What is your monthly income? Are you comfortably paying your bills and still have some money left over? Let's do an exercise. Get a piece of paper and do the math. Subtract your rent, mortgage, utilities, car payment, credit card payments, daycare expenses, groceries, etc. from your monthly income. When you have completed this task, you should have an idea of where you are financially. What do you

3

have left for the month, if anything? Are you overextended? Is your mortgage payment or rent taking up more than half of one paycheck? Are you in over your head on credit card debt? These are things that you have to take into account when it comes to becoming financially free. Most of America's problems come from the fact that we aren't making enough money for the times that we live in. Am I telling you to quit your job? No. But I am telling you that it's not the will of God for you to always be worried about money when there are problems you can easily resolve yourself.

You cannot fight today's devils with yesterday's anointing. *Matthew 6: 11-13 (NKJV)* "Give us this day our daily bread. And forgive us our debts, as we forgive our debtors. And do not lead us into temptation, but deliver us from the evil one. For Yours is the kingdom and the power and the glory forever. Amen." The Lord's Prayer is such a powerful passage of the Scripture. You have to take it and apply it to your life. You have to get some new insight, information, resources and make some changes if you want to survive in this evolving society that we live in. *John 15: 19 (KJB)* "If ye were of the world, the world would love his own: but because ye are not of the world, but I have chosen you out of the world, therefore the world hateth you." So as Christians, we have to get smarter about the financial commitments, agreements and decisions we make.

Financial freedom starts with making good, sound judgements without wavering in any way. If it doesn't feel right, don't do it; if it's taking up most of your income, it's time to rethink; if you're struggling to pay for it, something else needs to be done. Continuously evaluate yourself and let the Lord lead and guide you to areas where you need to make adjustments. Your financial freedom means more than you think. 1. Peace of mind 2. You can serve the Lord better 3. You can sow more into the work of the Lord and your local church 4. You have something saved for rainy days 5. Less stress, etc. Financial problems are one of the leading causes of certain illnesses and mental disorders. It's time to obtain your financial freedom through Christ.

WHAT DOES GOD SAY
ABOUT YOUR FINANCES?

The Lord is concerned with every aspect of your life including your finances. Jesus talks about money on several different occasions. And he also lets us know the importance of it.

Reference these Scriptures:

Hebrew 13: 5 (KJV)- [Let your] conversation [be] without covetousness; [and be] content with such things as ye have: for he hath said, I will never leave thee, nor forsake thee.

1 Timothy 6:10 (KJV) - For the love of money is the root of all evil: which while some coveted after, they have erred from the faith, and pierced themselves through with many sorrows.

Matthew 6:24 (KJV) - No man can serve two masters: for either he will hate the one, and love the other; or else he will hold to the one, and despise the other. Ye cannot serve God and mammon.

Ecclesiastes 5:10 (KJV) – He that loveth silver shall not be satisfied with silver; nor he that loveth abundance with increase: this [is] also vanity.

Proverbs 22:7 (KJV) – The rich ruleth over the poor, and the borrower [is] servant to the lender.

Matthew 6:31–33 (KJV) – Therefore take no thought, saying, What shall we eat? or, What shall we drink? or, Wherewithal shall we be clothed? (For after all these things do the Gentiles seek) for your heavenly Father knoweth that ye have need of all these things. But seek ye first the kingdom of God, and his righteousness; and all these things shall be added unto you.

Proverbs 13:11 (KJV) – Wealth [gotten] by vanity shall be diminished: but he that gathereth by labour shall increase.

Matthew 6:19–21 (KJV) – Lay not up for yourselves treasures upon earth, where moth and rust doth corrupt, and where thieves break through and steal:

Deuteronomy 8:18 (KJV)- But thou shalt remember the Lord thy God: for (it is) he that giveth thee power to get wealth, that he may establish his covenant which he sware unto thy fathers, as (it is) this day.

2 Corinthians 9:7 (KJV)- Every man according as he purposeth in his heart, (so let him give}; not grudgingly, or of necessity: for God loveth a cheerful giver.

Luke 12:33-34 (KJV) - Sell that ye have, and give alms; provide yourselves bags which wax not old, a treasure in the heavens that faileth not, where no thief approacheth, neither moth corrupteth. For where your treasure is, there will your heart be also.

Proverbs 13:22 (KJV) - A good [man] leaveth an inheritance to his children's children: and the wealth of the sinner [is] laid up for the just.

Luke 16:11 (KJV) – If therefore ye have not been faithful in the unrighteous mammon, who will commit to your trust the true [riches]?

Malachi 3:10 (KJV) – Bring ye all the tithes into the storehouse, that there may be meat in mine house, and prove me now herewith, saith the LORD of hosts, if I will not open you the windows of heaven, and pour you out a blessing, that [there shall] not [be room] enough [to receive it].

Deuteronomy 28: 1–14 (KJV)– And it shall come to pass, if thou shalt hearken diligently unto the voice of the Lord thy God, to observe and to do all his commandments which I command thee this day, that the Lord thy God will set thee on high above all nations of the earth: And all these blessings shall come on thee, and overtake thee, if thou shalt hearken unto the voice of the Lord thy God. Blessed shalt thou be in the city, and blessed shalt thou be in the field. Blessed shall be the fruit of thy body, and the fruit of thy ground, and the fruit of thy cattle, the increase of thy kind, and the flocks of thy sheep. Blessed shall be thy basket and thy store. Blessed shalt thou be when thou comest in, and blessed shalt thou be when thou goest out. The Lord shall cause thine enemies that rise up against thee to be smitten before thy face: they shall come out against thee one way, and flee before thee seven ways. The Lord shall command the blessing upon thee in thy storehouses, and in all that thou settest thine hand unto; and he shall bless thee in the land which the Lord thy God giveth thee. The Lord shall establish thee a holy people unto himself, as he hath sworn unto thee, if thou shalt keep the commandments of the Lord thy God, and walk in his ways. And all people of the earth shall see that thou art called by the name of the Lord; and they shall be afraid of thee. And the Lord shall make thee plenteous in goods, in the fruit of thy body, and in the fruit of thy cattle, and in the fruit of thy ground, in the land which the Lord sware unto thy fathers to give thee. The Lord shall open unto thee his good treasure, the heaven to give thee rain unto thy land in his season, and to bless all the work of thine hand: and thou shalt lend unto many nations, and thou shalt not borrow. And the Lord shall make thee the head, and not the tail; and thou shalt be above only, and thou shalt not be beneath; if that thou hearken unto the commandments of the Lord thy God, which I command thee this day, to observe and to do them: And thou shalt not go aside from any of the words which I command thee this day, to the right hand, or to the left, to go after other gods to serve them.

★★★★★

There are so many more scriptures about money. As you can see, the Lord is concerned about every aspect of you financially. I urge you to go back over the scriptures in your free time. The Amplified and NIV versions of the Bible are two very good sources for studying. They provide a clear understanding of the Scriptures. Just imagine if you were to get fortified in the Word of God with even more than the subject of money. Your life, thinking, finances, mentality, habits, buying habits, and decisions will all change for the better. This is your time, it's your season; this is your hour to become financially free.

DESTROYING THE
YOKE OF DEBT

Many of us have gotten ourselves neck deep into debts; from mortgage payments, credit cards, car payments, to rents and loans. "In today's economy, massive consumer debt has crippled the personal balance sheet of individuals around the country, making a tough economy even tougher. With foreclosures on the rise and many Americans crippled by over-extended credit cards, personal debt is becoming a major player in the economic crisis." (www.cnbc.com/2009/04/27/Americas-Biggest-Types-of-Debt-.html)

The yoke of debt has captivated many Christians, even churches with huge mortgage payments and not enough members to support the vision. I know pastors who have gotten into mortgage deals and used over $25,000 of their own personal credit cards to build their churches. We are living in an era when people have a 'right now' mentality. You want everything right now, irrespective of the cost.

It's time for the entrapment to stop and for the yoke to be destroyed. *Isaiah 10:27 (KJV)*. "And it shall come to pass in that day, that his burden shall be taken away from off thy shoulder, and his yoke from off thy neck, and the yoke shall be destroyed because of the anointing." It's not God's will for you to be enslaved in your finances. If more than half of your income goes out of your hand to pay some form of debt, you have to destroy the yoke now – those bills and problems and even some people who have attached themselves to you for the only purpose of draining your resources and the increase which the Lord has given you.

If you are always lacking and in need and you have a job or a source of income, it's time to cast lots as it was done in the book of Jonah. They wanted to know why they were going through so much trouble and so many problems and the issue was sitting right on the boat with them. Identify your problem and resolve it.

RISE ABOVE YOUR CURRENT FINANCIAL SITUATION AND SEIZE WHAT GOD HAS PROMISED YOU

As Christians, many of us have ideas, visions, dreams and things we would like to accomplish. More often than not, you need seed money to sow into your vision. The Lord has promised to bless you but you have to remember *Luke 14:28 (KJV)*, "For which of you, intending to build a tower, sitteth not down first, and counteth the cost, whether he have sufficient to finish it?"

This scripture is very significant and immediately lets you know money is needed when you're trying to accomplish something. There are times when the Lord will bless in a supernatural way and you won't need money. But for the most part, finances are needed. In the previous section, we spoke about destroying the yoke of debt so you can move forward. The extra money you save from destroying your yoke can be invested in your vision and what He has called you to do. For the most part, it will cost you something to seize some of the promises of God. It's time for the financial limitations to be taken off of your life.

If we are going to move into the next dimension and phase of our lives, we have to become good stewards of what the Lord is giving us. Times are getting harder; the economy is not the way it used to be; people are losing their jobs here and there; most are giving up, committing suicide because of a lack of money to pay their bills. But we ought to be like Joseph when he stored up things, so he was prepared when the famine came. What do you have saved in case of an emergency? If something major were to happen right now and you had to pack light and move fast, could you do it? It would be wise to at least save 10 percent of your income to be prepared for any type of unexpected occurrences. The car may need to be repaired, the hot water heater could break, any life circumstances can put you in a bad situation if you're not well prepared for them.

The information provided to you in this resource is to educate, enlighten and open up your eyes to the truth about finances.

THE COMING OUT STAGE

The coming out stage is by far the most difficult part of obtaining financial freedom. The word of God reminds us that, in *Philippians 4:13 (KJV)*, "I can do all things through Christ who strengthens me." So in other words, you can get through your financial problems through Christ.

Your coming out may require you to file bankruptcy if you are in over your head and just can't afford to pay, it may be advantageous for you to consult with an attorney who specializes in bankruptcy. They can provide you with information so you can judge if it's the best option for your situation.

For those individuals who are in the position to make some kind of payment arrangements, it would be great if you can call your creditors and start making arrangements that you can afford to pay on a monthly or biweekly basis.

If you don't have the knowledge for making arrangements with your creditors or settlements, we have many years of experience in this Industry and can possibly be of some assistance to you. Now is the time to get your credit report cleaned up from mistakes that were made in the past. Most people don't just stop paying their bills. Some situations or circumstances caused you to fall behind and eventually caused you to give up on paying altogether. But there is still hope. Through Prayer, Fasting and making payment arrangements on your debts, you should see positive results from your efforts. You cannot just sit and watch everything fall apart around you any longer. It's time for a change and it's God's will that you recover all. Recovery is not always an easy process. When you make up your mind to take the bull by the horn, you have to be serious about it and expect the enemy to fight you. Keep in mind that the Lord is with thee. Stay positive, focused and keep moving until you reach your financial goals.

I hope that the information provided in this source has challenged you to become financially free. I invite you to join a local church where you can grow in God and accept the Lord Jesus Christ as your personal saviour, if you have not done so yet.

Visit the website @ www.lekiesha.com
Book your Strategy Conference
for your Church or Ministry.

WIN THE GAME

THE END